The Work People Do
FARMER

The Work People Do
FARMER

by Betsy Imershein

JULIAN MESSNER

ACKNOWLEDGMENTS

Many people graciously allowed me to photograph them at their work on Blooming Hill Organic Farm. I particularly want to thank Guy, Peggy and Travis Jones who own Blooming Hill—for permitting me to photograph them and their farm and for answering my innumerable questions. Their workers: Lucy Axton, Michelle Bouchard, Rahel Buxbaum, Charlie Ghook, Ajila Hart, Barney Hill, Cindy Jones, Drew Kissinger, Christina Knight, Lisa Kotraba, David Lipton, Jeff Lobb, Will Margitan, Sondra Pugh, Cynthia Wozniak, and Anne Marie Zuppani were helpful, patient and cheerful as I photographed them working and I thank each and every one.

I would also like to thank Hall Gibson of Ryder Farm in Brewster, NY and Susan and Ted Blew of Blew Farm in Pittstown, NJ for taking the time to speak with me and show me around their farms. Lorraine Caruso offered great help as did my husband, Jim—I thank them, and Robin Cohen, too.

Several organizations work to help the farmer survive and the consumer have better produce to eat. I would like to mention and thank three of them. Each depends on consumer interest and support to work most effectively and would be most happy to answer your questions and accept your help and contributions:

Greenmarket—c/o Council on the Environment of New York City,
51 Chambers Street, New York, NY 10007 (212) 566-0990;

Farm Aid, 21 Erie Street, Cambridge, MA 02139 (617) 354-2922;

Natural Organic Farmers Association of NY, PO Box 454,
Ithaca, NY 14851 (607) 648-5557.

The Work People Do

ANIMAL DOCTOR

AUTO MECHANIC

FARMER

JULIAN MESSNER and colophon are trademarks of Simon & Schuster, Inc.
Design by Michèle Goycoolea and Sylvia Frezzolini.
Manufactured in the United States of America.

Lib. ed. 10 9 8 7 6 5 4 3 2 1   Paper ed. 10 9 8 7 6 5 4 3 2 1

Library of Congress Cataloging-in-Publication Data
Imershein, Betsy.   Farmer / by Betsy Imershein.—(The work people do)   Summary: Describes the work on an organic farm, including the weeding, care of livestock, and field work.   1. Farmers—Juvenile literature.   2. Farm life—Juvenile literature.   3. Organic farming—Juvenile literature.   4. Agriculture—Vocational guidance—Juvenile literature.   [1. Farm life.   2. Organic farming.   3. Occupations.]
I. Title.   II. Series.   S519.I44   1990   630—dc20   89-13578   CIP   AC
ISBN 0-671-68185-0 (lib. bdg.)
ISBN 0-671-68188-5 (pbk.)

To Marla,
for her nurturing and support

Guy and Peggy are farmers. They grow fruits, vegetables, flowers, and herbs on a small farm called Blooming Hill. They live here with their son, Travis.

Guy bought the land for their farm ten years ago. He cleared it of grass and many of its trees and started planting. Peggy joined him about five years later.

For Guy and Peggy, farming offers variety in their work and many challenges. It's honest physical labor, done outdoors in cooperation with nature. And they share the work of the farm.

Until Travis was born, Peggy worked in the
fields every day. Now when she's out in the fields,
Travis is usually with her. He helps pick the
strawberries and feed Daisy, the cow.

Several other people work and live at the farm
during the growing season. Some, like Ann Marie,
want to have a farm of their own someday. She is
learning about farming by working for Guy and
Peggy. Others, like Michelle and Drew, enjoy
working on a farm during their summer break
from college.

Anyone who loves the land and loves working on it can be a farmer. Some people study farming in college; some teach themselves how to be farmers, as Peggy and Guy did; and others are farmers because their families have been farmers for a very long time.

Blooming Hill is an organic farm. That means that no chemicals are put on the crops to feed the plants, kill the bugs and weeds, or prevent disease. Organic farmers, like Peggy and Guy, rely on nature's fertilizers, or foods, and other natural means to grow healthy and good crops.

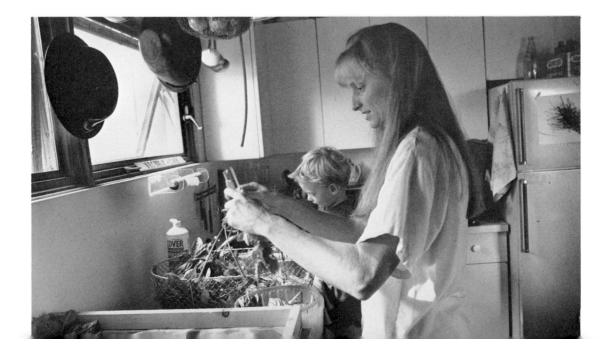

Each day Peggy and Guy have a list of things that need to be done for their crops. Peggy does some work in the fields and selects at least one project such as drying herbs or canning vegetables. Guy's list revolves around what needs to be plowed, planted, harvested, cut, and fixed.

At least one day is set aside each week for weeding. Since the crops are not sprayed on organic farms, weeds grow as well as the vegetables and fruit. If the weeds aren't pulled, they rob the plants of the moisture and nutrients necessary to grow and be healthy.

15

16

In addition to work related to their growing and taking care of the crops, many tasks must be done to take care of the farm. Guy is an electrician, carpenter, and mechanic, while Peggy handles all the finances.

Another chore that must be done every day is taking care of the chickens and rooster. Travis feeds them and helps Guy fix their coop when it needs repairs. The chickens provide Guy and Peggy and their helpers with a few fresh eggs each day.

They also have several bee hives to provide honey. Guy and Peggy do not take care of the bees but have someone come to check on them every few weeks. Charlie works nearby and knows a lot about beekeeping. When he comes, he usually brings some helpers.

The weather plays a big part in farm life, and because it is unpredictable, planning ahead is not easy to do. This spring it rained a great deal. The ground was so wet that many of the vegetables were planted later than usual and it was difficult to cut hay.

Hay is used as food for animals and it must last all winter long. Guy needs at least three dry days for the job to get done right. If it rains on the hay before it is baled, or bundled, then it will spoil. Guy did cut some hay in the spring, but with all the rain, none has been cut since. It's the beginning of August before he can cut more.

Guy puts a special attachment onto the tractor when he cuts hay. The hay sits on the field for two days to dry. Then it is baled and put in trucks for later storage or delivery to eager customers.

Guy and Peggy farm intensively. This means that the vegetables are grown close together and some of the fields are planted several times in the same growing season. By planting so often, their small farm produces an unending supply of vegetables and fruit from spring until late fall.

This is important, for Peggy and Guy sell their
produce at a greenmarket in a nearby city. Peggy
goes to the market on Wednesday and Guy goes
on Friday from May until Christmas. It is the main
source of their income.

Several days each week the fruit and vegetables
and flowers and herbs need to be harvested, or
picked, for market. Guy and Peggy supervise their
workers as well as harvest the crops themselves.

Harvesting is a long, slow process because
everything at Blooming Hill is done by hand. Guy
cuts each flower and each squash individually
with a knife. Ann Marie, Michelle, and Drew
bunch and pick the herbs.

Everything is washed at least once to get off the dust and dirt. Guy bunches the vegetables together to make them ready for sale. Then Drew takes all the produce to cold storage where it is kept overnight for Peggy or Guy to take to the market.

Market days are early days. Ann Marie and
Peggy get up around four o'clock in the morning
to load the truck and drive to the city. Once there,
setting up usually takes quite a bit of time. Often,
customers come before all the food is out of the
truck. Many are regular customers who tell Peggy
and Guy how delicious their food is and how
much they look forward to the market days.

Farming is a hard life. Peggy and Guy are up with the sun each day to get all their work done. And each growing season has its hardships and rewards when some crops do better than expected while others do not. But it is a life filled with satisfactions, of nurturing the crops till harvest and enjoying the pleasures their customers take in eating their produce. They wouldn't want to do anything else.

ABOUT THE AUTHOR

BETSY IMERSHEIN grew up in New York and holds a master's degree in social work from Yeshiva University. She studied photography at the International Center of Photography, Parsons School of Design, Cooper Union and the Center for Nature Photography.

Ms. Imershein's other books include: *When You Go To Kindergarten,* published in 1986; *Animal Doctor,* published in 1988; *Auto Mechanic,* published in 1989; and *Finding Red/Finding Yellow,* published in 1989. She lives with her husband, James Howe, and daughter Zoe in Hastings-on-Hudson, New York.